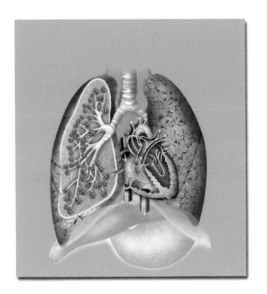

The Heart and Lungs

Ben Williams

Table of Contents

A Busy Place

The world is a busy place. People work, play, and go, go, go. Over here and over there, something is always happening.

The outside world is very busy.

But there is another busy world, one that you can not see. Inside of you, under your skin, your body never stops going. Blood goes through your body. Air goes in and out.

Yes, your *inside* world is very busy, too!

An Important Team

In the middle of all this activity, resting snugly inside your chest, are your heart and lungs. They are an important team! They work together every moment of every day to send your body the oxygen and nutrition it needs. They take good care of you, so you must be sure to take good care of them!

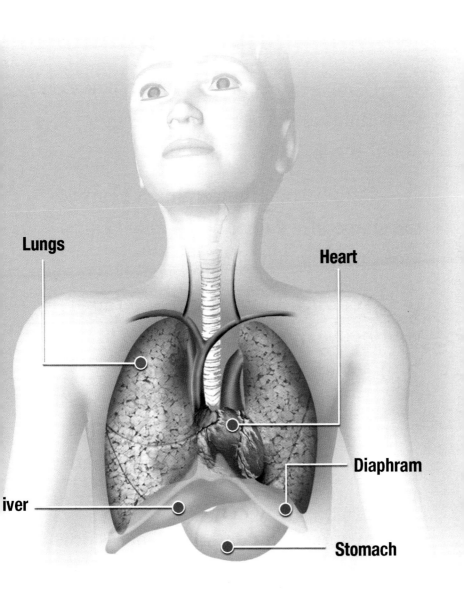

Lungs

Heart

Diaphram

iver

Stomach

The Heart and How It Works

Your heart is in your chest, between your lungs and just left of the center. It is about the size of a closed fist.

People sometimes think a heart is the shape of a valentine. A real heart looks nothing like that.

Your heart pumps blood through your body. Blood brings oxygen to your body's cells. Living things need oxygen or they will die. Once your cells receive the oxygen, the blood returns to your heart to get more. Then your blood is pumped out again.

In and out, in and out. That is how your heart pumps your blood.

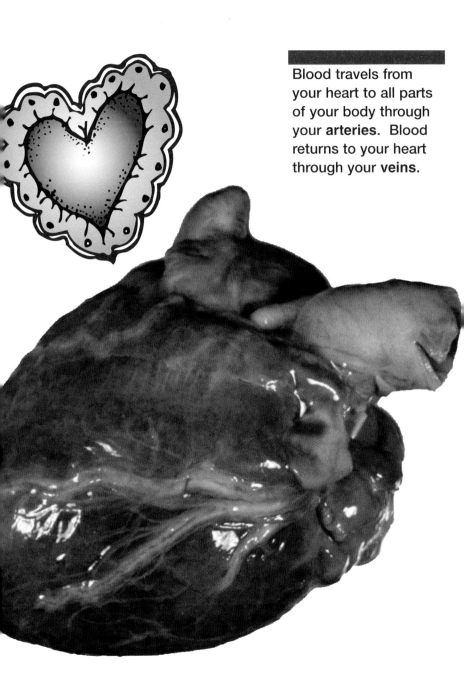

Blood travels from your heart to all parts of your body through your **arteries**. Blood returns to your heart through your **veins**.

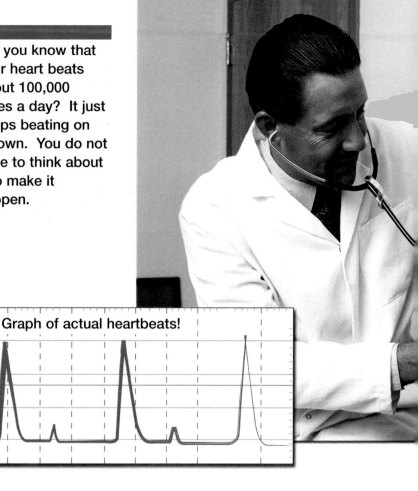

Did you know that your heart beats about 100,000 times a day? It just keeps beating on its own. You do not have to think about it to make it happen.

Graph of actual heartbeats!

Place your hand over your heart. Do you feel something? It is your heartbeat. Your heart beats as it pumps the blood.

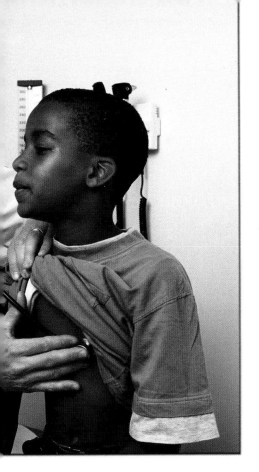

It is impossible to place your ear against your chest to hear your heartbeat. So, you can use a **stethescope**. A stethescope is a special instrument with two ear pieces connected to a long tube and a flat piece at the end. If the flat piece is held against your chest and the ear pieces are placed in your ears, you can hear your heartbeat very clearly.

Your heart beats in a pattern of two. If you heard the sound of your heartbeat, the first beat would sound dull and the second beat would sound sharp. It would sound like this: thump THUMP, thump THUMP.

9

How does your heart work?

Look at the diagram. Blood enters your heart from your lungs. Your heart pumps the blood into your arteries. Once the oxygen is delivered, your veins carry the blood back to your heart. Then out the blood goes into your lungs for a fresh supply of oxygen.

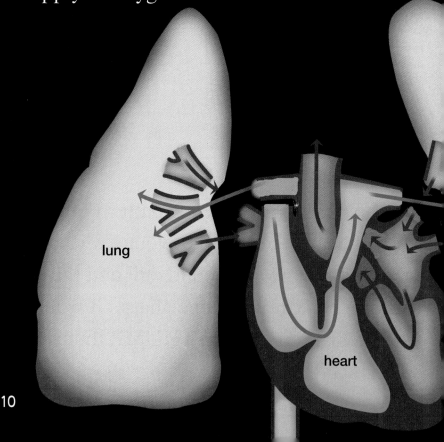

lung

heart

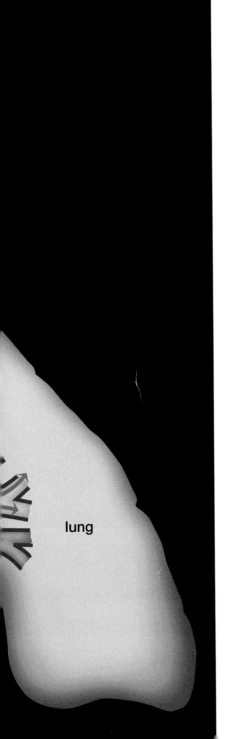

lung

Your heart is like a pump that moves blood through your body every second of every day. This is called **circulation.**

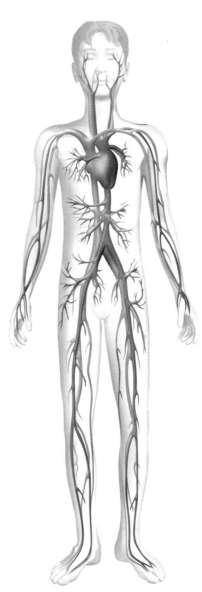

What happens if the heart becomes sick? A body can not work well with a sick heart. You must take good care of your heart to keep your whole body strong.

The Lungs and How They Work

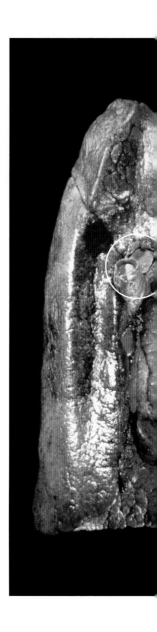

Your two lungs are in your chest on either side of your heart. They look like soft, wet, pink-gray sponges.

Breathe in deeply and you can see your chest rise. That is because your lungs are filling with air. Breathe out and your chest lowers. It is releasing the air.

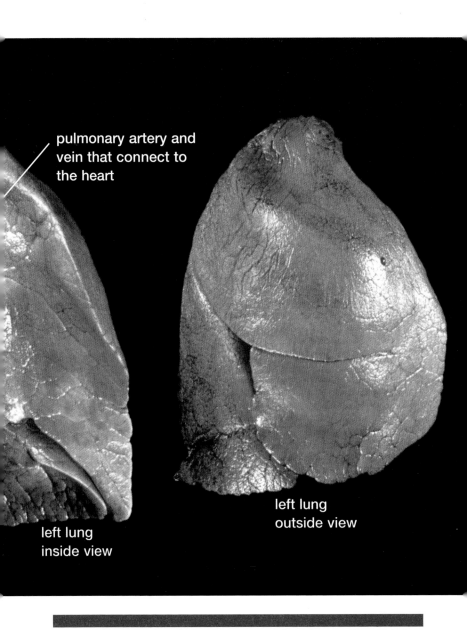

pulmonary artery and vein that connect to the heart

left lung
inside view

left lung
outside view

Just like with your heartbeat, you do not need to think about breathing. Your body just breathes on its own.

Why do you need to breathe? You breathe to get oxygen. Air is breathed into your nose and down your **trachea**. Your trachea carries the air through tubes that look like the branches of an upside-down tree. The tubes are called **bronchi**. They take the oxygen from the air and send it to your blood.

Your body knows how much air it needs. If you run hard or get scared, you will breathe faster to get more oxygen.

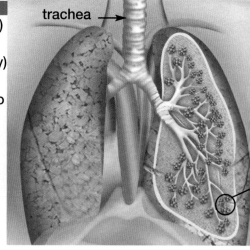

Your **trachea** (TRA-kēy-uh) is also called a windpipe. Your **bronchi** (BRONG-key) look like two long branches. They break into smaller branches called **bronchioles** (BRONG-ki-uls). At the ends of the bronchioles are tiny air sacks called alveoli (al-VE-o-li).

trachea →

We breathe in oxygen. We breathe out carbon dioxide.

How often do you breathe? You breathe about 15 breaths a minute and more than 20,000 breaths a day!

alveoli

bronchioles

When you breathe, your nose and lungs work together to moisten, warm, and clean the air. Your lungs only want pure, fresh oxygen.

You **inhale** (breathe in) to get **oxygen** into your body. You **exhale** (breathe out) to get rid of gases like **carbon dioxide** that you do not need. When you inhale, the muscles around your lungs pull your lungs down. This makes the lungs bigger inside and lets them suck in air. When you exhale, your muscles relax and your lungs go back to their normal size. This forces the gases out of your body.

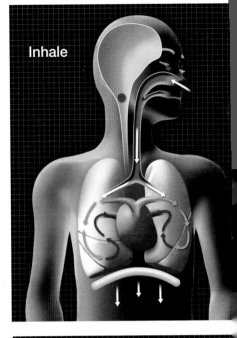

Inhale

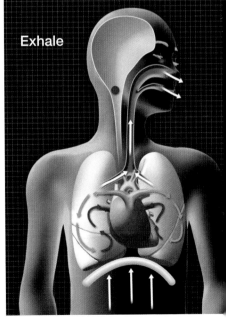

Exhale

Since there is oxygen in water, why can fish breathe underwater but we can not? Fish have gills that take oxygen from the water for them. We do not have gills. We can only get our oxygen from the air or with the help of special equipment.

A Healthy Heart and Lungs

What can you do to take good care of your heart and lungs? Here are some important things to remember to keep them healthy and strong.

- Eat right. Healthy food means a healthy heart and lungs.
- Exercise every day. It keeps your heart and lungs strong.
- Get plenty of rest. Rest helps your heart and lungs get the energy they need.
- See your doctor for check-ups. Then you can be sure that your heart and lungs are well.
- Be happy! A good attitude helps to keep your heart and lungs healthy.
- Do not smoke! Smoking damages your heart and lungs and makes them work much too hard.

When you take good care of yourself, you help yourself to live a long time. You might even live to be 122! That is the oldest known age for a human. Here is a graph to show the oldest known age for the six animals, including human, that live the longest.

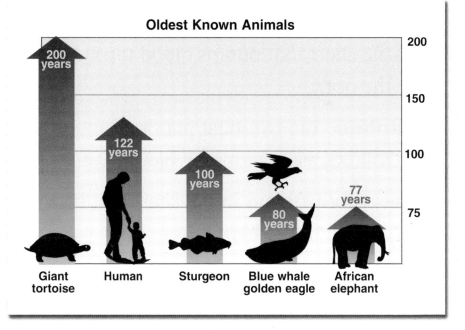

Oldest Known Animals

Glossary

blood   the fluid that moves through the body's veins and arteries

breath   the air a person breathes in and out

breathe   to take in and release air

exercise   body activity

heart   body organ near the center of the chest that pumps blood through the body

heartbeat   the two-beat pattern the heart follows when pumping blood

lungs   body organs in the chest that bring oxygen to the blood

oxygen   a colorless, tasteless, and odorless gas that the human body needs to live

pump   to force a liquid from one space to another